Kings
&
Queens
OF ENGLAND

Written by Louise Jones
Illustrated by Robin Davies

ABOUT THIS BOOK

The story of how each of England's kings and queens came to rule
the kingdom is told in the captivating words and pictures of
Kings and Queens of England.
The major dramatic events of each reign
are featured in the main text.
Additional pictures and captions in the margins of the book
expand the full, rich picture of times past – from England's
first great Saxon king, Alfred, to the problems
and misdoings of Richard III.
The foldout family tree shows the relationships between
different monarchs.

Main illustrations by Robin Davies
Portrait illustrations by Jon Jackson

Ladybird books are widely available, but in case of
difficulty may be ordered by post or telephone from:

Ladybird Books – Cash Sales Department
Littlegate Road Paignton Devon TQ3 3BE
Telephone 01803 554761

A catalogue record for this book is available
from the British Library

Published by Ladybird Books Ltd Loughborough Leicestershire UK

CONTENTS

CELTS

LOTHIAN

BERNICIA

NORTHUMBRIA

York

Offa's Dyke

MERCIA

CELTS

EAST ANGLIA

ESSEX

Athelney Chippenham London

WESSEX Winchester KENT

CELTS SUSSEX

Hastings

The kingdoms of Saxon Britain.

Offa's Dyke. In the 8th century, Offa, the Saxon king of Mercia (who called himself 'King of the English'), drove the Celts into Wales. He built an earthen wall 240 kilometres (150 miles) long, with a ditch, to keep them there. The Welsh word for the English, 'seis', like the Scotch 'sassenach', really means 'Saxon'.

In the centuries before the arrival of the Romans, Britain was not ruled as one nation, but was divided among many separate tribes, who lived in the forests that covered most of England. The Celtic tribes of Britain chose their kings (or chieftains) by election. If a king did not act fairly and look after his people, he was **deposed** and replaced by a new king.

The Romans ruled Britain between 43 and 410. Celtic rule was restored after the Romans left, but by then many Celts were Christian. Towards the end of the Roman period, warlike invaders (Saxons, Angles and Jutes) attacked the east coast of Britain. They came from Germany and Denmark.

When the Romans left, the Saxons (as the Celts called all these invaders)

settled in Britain, and took most of southern England. They drove the Celts back to the far north (Scotland) and west (Wales and Cornwall). Then, as the Celts had, the Saxons divided England into kingdoms. At different times, powerful kings of particular kingdoms ruled the whole country.

From the 790s onwards, Viking raiders came from Scandinavia in longships: killing, **plundering** and taking slaves. Around 860 the Vikings formed an army, to conquer Britain, and took possession of large areas of England. By 870 only the Saxon kingdom of **Wessex** remained unconquered. Wessex, under a great Saxon leader, Alfred, held out against the Viking invaders. It is with Alfred that the story of the kings and queens of England really begins.

Viking invaders. The Saxons had been violent in their invasions. The Vikings were even more violent.

Arthur in battle. Early historians tell of a great Celtic leader called Arthur. He defeated the Saxons many times in the 6th century.

ALFRED THE GREAT
871-899 (b. 849)

ALFRED THE GREAT

Alfred was the youngest of the five warrior sons of Ethelwulf, the Saxon King of Wessex. In 870 he proved himself a great warrior, fighting the Danes. Because of this, in 871 the people chose him as king. That year Alfred fought the Danish invaders nine times. He fortified the kingdom of Wessex, formed a navy, and organised his army so that half guarded the kingdom while the other half farmed.

In 877 the Danes attacked Alfred's palace at Chippenham, Wiltshire, and he fled to the Athelney marshes in Somerset. The following year, Alfred broke out of hiding and retook his palace at the Battle of Edington, Wiltshire. He made peace with the Danes and agreed that they should rule East Anglia, while he could concentrate on ruling southern England. Guthrum, the Danish

The 'Alfred' jewel. This gold and enamel jewel has the inscription: 'Alfred ordered me to be made'. It is probably the head of a bone or ivory pointer, used to point to words when reading. Alfred sent out pointers with his newly-translated books.

leader, took Christian baptism, and Alfred was his sponsor (godfather).

In 885 Alfred invited Asser, a great Celtic scholar and priest, to work for him. Asser taught Alfred Latin and helped him to devise a system of just laws. Alfred became a learned king and won the respect of the Celts. He had great books translated into **Anglo-Saxon**, and he founded schools. His chief law was, 'Do not do to others what you would not want done to you.' Alfred is the only English monarch to be called 'the Great'.

Alfred and Asser. Alfred was a wise man, with great common sense. This was shown in his employing the Celtic scholar, Asser, as his teacher and adviser.

A burh. Alfred built many fortified towns, called 'burhs', to defend his kingdom. Deep ditches and banks of earth were set round them.

EDWARD (the Elder)
899-924 (b. 870)
ATHELSTAN
924-939 (b. 895)
EDMUND
(the Magnificent)
939-946 (b. 920)
EDRED 946-955 (b. 923)
EDWY 955-959 (b. 941)

Alfred's son, Edward the Elder, spent most of his reign fighting to push back the **frontiers** of the **Danelaw** (the Viking part of England).

Edward's eldest son, the handsome King Athelstan, was a hero who fought Vikings and Celts. He formed England into roughly the area it occupies today. Athelstan was the first of his family who could read and write from childhood. He was **devout**, and he drew up good laws.

In 937 Athelstan defeated a combined Danish and Celtic force at the Battle of Brunanburh, north Yorkshire. Fifty years later it was still commonly referred to as 'the great battle'.

Athelstan was the most powerful British ruler since the Romans, and he brought peace and unity. Many

Ethelfleda in battle. From 917 to 918 Edward's sister Ethelfleda, Queen of Mercia, led her forces into battle in his support. By 918, when Ethelfleda died, she and Edward ruled most of England.

Athelstan receiving a foreign ambassador. He was the first Anglo-Saxon king to rule the whole of England. He was known and admired throughout the Christian world. Foreign rulers sent him gifts, and asked his permission to take his sisters as their wives.

foreign kings sent him gifts, and poets came to sing his praises.

Athelstan's brothers, Edmund and Edred, spent their reigns strengthening the gains Athelstan had made. Edwy, Edmund's teenage son, was foolish and irresponsible. He is best remembered for banishing the wise Dunstan, Abbot of Glastonbury. This was because when Edwy left his coronation feast to visit his fiancée, Dunstan tried to persuade him to return. Edwy was eventually forced off the throne by the rulers of Mercia and Northumberland.

A coin of Athelstan's reign. He passed the first English laws controlling the issue of coinage, with severe penalties for **counterfeiters**.

EDGAR (the Peaceful)
959-975 (b. 942)
EDWARD (the Martyr)
975-978 (b. 962)
**ETHELRED I I
(the Unready)**
978-1013, 1014-1016
(b. 968)
SWEYN (Forkbeard)
1013-1014 (b. 960)

Six sub-kings (mostly Celts) pay tribute to Edgar's power by rowing him across the River Dee. This was in 973, the year he was crowned 'King of the Anglo-Saxon Empire'.

The reign of Edgar, Edwy's brother and successor, was a 'golden age'. Edgar recalled Dunstan, Abbot of Glastonbury, from exile, and made him Archbishop of Canterbury. Edgar gathered allies to help keep the peace, and was loved and honoured.

Edgar's son, Edward, was different: he was selfish and his reign was a disaster. Edward was murdered, and his 10-year-old stepbrother, Ethelred, was made king.

Ethelred did no better. He was lazy and unlucky, and useless in battle.

Danes had now become part of English society, but in 1002 Ethelred ordered that all Danes in England be killed. His order was not fully carried out; but this was an early example of racial persecution.

Ethelred's nickname, 'the Unready', was a pun on his name: 'Aethel-raed' means 'wise advice' in Anglo-Saxon; 'un-raed' means 'no advice' or 'bad advice'.

A comet in 975 was seen as a bad omen for the new king Edward's reign. In 976 there was famine. This was followed by rioting and bloodshed; many monasteries were destroyed.

When a huge Viking force harried the south coast of England in 1009, Ethelred told his people to pray and fast to make their enemies go away. He also had a coin minted with the Lamb of God (Jesus Christ) and the Dove (the Holy Spirit) on it, in the hope that this would help.

By 1011 the Danes held most of southeastern England. Ethelred paid them huge amounts of **Danegeld**, but they took more and more. In 1013 the Danish prince, Sweyn, invaded England and regained the north. Ethelred fled to Normandy, in northern France, leaving Sweyn to rule as king.

In 1014, after Sweyn died, the English asked Ethelred to return as their king. They did not want another Dane, Sweyn's son Cnut, to take the throne. Ethelred tried to punish Cnut's supporters in battle, but the attempt was a disaster and war broke out. Cnut pursued Ethelred to London to attack him. Ethelred died of natural causes, and the English accepted Cnut as king.

EDMUND (Ironside)
Apr-Nov 1016 (b. 989)
CNUT
1016-1035 (b. 995)
**HAROLD I
(Harefoot)** 1035-1040
(b. 1016)
HARTHACNUT
1040-1042 (b. 1018)

After Ethelred died in 1016, some people wanted Edmund, his son, to become king. Others preferred Cnut. A compromise was reached, and Cnut agreed to share England with Edmund (known as Edmund Ironside because of his courage and glamour). Seven months after Ethelred's death, Edmund died, and so in 1016 Cnut became king of all England. By 1030 he was king of Denmark and Norway too.

Cnut worked hard to keep hold of his lands. He was a peaceful, devoutly Christian monarch.

In 1035 Cnut died. He left two sons, Harold Harefoot and Harthacnut. They were half-brothers, and they hated each other.

Cnut meant Harthacnut to be king of England after him, but Harold took control of the country while Harthacnut was in Denmark.

Cnut and Edmund Ironside swear brotherhood. The two agreed to govern half of the country each. Cnut took the north and Edmund took Wessex – but Edmund was dead within a month of this agreement.

Harold did not live long, and Harthacnut spent his time as king punishing the people who had helped Harold.

Harthacnut was the last of the Danish **dynasty** founded by Cnut.

Cnut and the sea. It is said that Cnut told the rising tide to stop, to show his silly, flattering courtiers that his power was far less than God's power.

After Harold's death, Harthacnut had his half-brother's body dug up and thrown into a marsh.

EDWARD
(the Confessor)
1042-1066 (b. 1004)
HAROLD II
(Godwinson)
Jan-Oct 1066 (b. 1020)

Ethelred's son, Edward the Confessor, had a long and peaceful reign. His gentle manners and devotion to prayer and churchgoing earned him the nickname 'Confessor'.

Under the Danish kings, England had been divided among the **earls**. Wessex, home of earlier English kings, was now ruled by the powerful and ambitious Earl Godwin.

Godwin died in 1053. In 1056 his son, Harold, went to Europe for King Edward, to find Edmund Ironside's son, and make him Edward's heir. But in 1057 this new heir died. Harold went to Europe again. This time he told Edward's second cousin, Duke William of Normandy, that Edward wanted him to be the next king of England. But, when Edward died in 1066, he said Harold should be king.

Harold was a fine soldier; he held off an attack by Edward's exiled brother Tostig, and settled

EDWARD'S BURIAL

KING HAROLD

WILLIAM SAILS TO ENGLAND

The Bayeux Tapestry. It was made about 1070 and tells the story of Harold and William the Conqueror, rather like a cartoon strip. Not many people could read at that time, so it was necessary to tell the story in pictures.

an army in the Isle of Wight, expecting Duke William to attack. They waited, bored, for months. Harvest time came and many left to gather the harvest.

William planned to sail in August, but had to wait for a favourable wind. In September, Tostig, with Harald Hardrada, King of Norway, attacked York, in the north of England. Harold rushed north and beat the invaders on 25 September, 1066 at Stamford Bridge, near York. Three days later Duke William landed near Hastings, on the south coast. Harold rode south, gathering troops as he went. William attacked before the English army was ready. The Normans were well rested and on 14 October, 1066 Harold and most of his men died after fighting heroically at Senlac, near Hastings.

Ethelred's great-grandson, Edgar, was chosen king, but never crowned. William marched on London, **ravaging** the country. A party of elders met him and offered him the crown.

The 'shield wall' used by English soldiers. This made it very difficult for the enemy to wound them.

The Bayeux Tapestry is an embroidery on linen. It is 63 metres long (207 feet), and is kept in the French town of Bayeux, Normandy. It was probably made in England.

BATTLE OF HASTINGS

HAROLD'S DEATH

**WILLIAM I
(the Conqueror)**
1066-1087 (b. 1027)

Serfs working on their lord's land. William brought the feudal system from Normandy. Society was divided into groups. The lowest, the serfs, lived on the land but did not own it, and were compelled to work for their lords.

William was crowned on Christmas Day 1066, in Westminster Abbey. He strengthened Edward the Confessor's legal system, and made England into a **feudal society**. He punished rebels by taking their land, which he gave to his Norman barons. By 1085, only two of the large landowners were Anglo-Saxon.

Some Saxons did resist Norman rule. Hereward the Wake was one. He became a great Saxon hero, who led uprisings against the Normans. He was eventually outlawed and fled into hiding in the marshes of Lincolnshire, where others joined him. It is not known what happened to him, but his name became legendary.

In 1086, William listed all English land and property, with its ownership, for tax purposes. In later years his famous survey became known as 'The Domesday Book'.

William left England to his middle son, called William Rufus, who was his favourite. Robert, the eldest son, became Duke of Normandy, and Henry, the youngest, inherited a fortune. William died in France in 1087 of injuries received when his horse threw him while he was fighting the King of France. William was buried at Caen, in Normandy.

A Norman arch. The Normans brought their language and culture to England. They were descended from Vikings who had settled in northern France since 911.

The Domesday Book. People began calling it this because, like the Day of Judgment, there could be no appeal against what it contained. (Doom meant 'judgment'.)

WILLIAM II (Rufus)
1087-1100 (b. 1056)
HENRY I (Beauclerc)
1100-1135 (b. 1068)

WILLIAM II AND HENRY I

William Rufus was a brave fighter and a practical king, who spent much of his reign trying to win Normandy from his older brother, Robert. Henry, the third and youngest brother, sided with William and Robert in turn. In 1091 William and Robert made peace; but their **treaty** collapsed after William broke his promise to help Robert in battle. In 1096 Robert 'lent' Normandy to William in return for 10,000 marks (a very large sum of money, equivalent to about £6,500), while Robert went on a **Crusade**.

Whether William would have given Normandy back we do not know, for in 1100 he died. His younger brother, Henry, was crowned within days. Henry promised to maintain peace and justice, and he worked hard at running England more efficiently. He loved the Church and encouraged learning; at that time the two were connected, because most books were written and copied out

A motte and bailey castle. This was the earliest type of Norman castle. The 'motte' was the mound on which the wooden keep, the strong central part of the castle, was built.

The 'bailey' was a fenced area where the household lived, and storerooms and workshops were located. By 1100 William had fortified the Kingdom of England with over 5,000 castles.

by monks. Because of this, Henry was nicknamed 'Beauclerc' ('good scholar' in French). In 1101, Henry gave most of Normandy back to Robert, to stop him from trying to take the English throne. The brothers remained enemies, however, and in 1106 Henry defeated Robert at the Battle of Tinchebrai, Normandy. Robert was Henry's prisoner for the rest of his life, and Henry ruled Normandy. Henry was the only one of the three brothers to marry. He had twins, William and Matilda; he also had a favourite nephew, Stephen of Blois. In 1120 his son William was drowned in a shipwreck, and Matilda became the heir to the English throne. When her husband, the **Holy Roman Emperor**, died, Henry married her to Geoffrey Plantagenet, Count of Anjou, by whom she had three sons. In 1135 Geoffrey angered Henry by asking for part of Normandy, but Henry died before their quarrel was resolved.

The sinking of the 'White Ship'. Henry's son, William, was on this ship when it was wrecked in 1120. William was drowned.

Fountains Abbey, North Yorkshire, England. Henry built magnificent abbeys; some are now in ruins but still beautiful.

STEPHEN

Before he died, Henry I had said that Matilda, his daughter, should succeed him. This was unusual as women did not normally rule in England. Matilda was unpopular, and there were many who were against her becoming queen.

When Henry died, the throne was offered to Matilda's cousin, Stephen of Blois. He had been living at his uncle Henry's court, and was liked by the people, for his courage and good nature. On 22 December, 1135, Stephen was crowned king. He was not a wise king, and in 1138 civil war began as Earl Robert of Gloucester, Henry I's eldest **illegitimate** son, led a rebellion aimed at making Matilda queen. She came to England from France in 1139, and in 1141 Stephen

Matilda. By her second marriage she was Countess of Anjou. But her first husband, who had died, had been the Holy Roman Emperor, and she preferred to call herself 'Empress Matilda'. Her son Henry by her second marriage (later Henry II) was known as 'Henry Fitzempress' (Henry, son of the empress), rather than 'Henry of Anjou'.

was imprisoned. Matilda was chosen queen, but her greedy actions angered the people so much that she was not crowned, and was driven out of London. Civil war raged for eight more years. Then in 1147, Earl Robert of Gloucester died, and Matilda fled.

Stephen remained a weak king. Matilda's husband, Geoffrey Plantagenet, did well, becoming Duke of Normandy in 1144. In 1153 their son, Henry, invaded England. Stephen's own son, Eustace, died, and Stephen made peace with Henry Plantagenet by declaring him heir to the throne.

Stephen and the little hostage.
In 1152 the leader of a castle Stephen was attacking asked for a truce. Stephen was given a five-year-old boy as a **hostage**. The truce was broken but, Stephen spared the boy although he had been urged to catapult the boy back into the castle. The boy later recalled playing 'knights' – a game like conkers – with King Stephen, using plantain stalks he had picked from the grass.

HENRY II
1154-1189 (b. 1133)

HENRY II

Henry II was the great-grandson of William the Conqueror. He also ruled the French regions of Normandy, Aquitaine, Anjou, and Maine. He was the first of the Plantagenet kings. The name 'plantagenet' is from the Latin *planta genesta*, which means broom. Henry's father (Geoffrey of Anjou) loved hunting so much that he planted broom all over his land to encourage game to breed and live in its cover. It is also said that he wore a sprig of broom in his helmet.

Henry II was highly intelligent, active, efficient, and hot-tempered. Aquitaine and Maine were Henry's through his marriage

Thomas Becket's murder. Becket was Henry's friend. But after Henry made him Archbishop of Canterbury, he resisted Henry's attempts to reduce the Church's power. In 1170, Henry, in a rage, begged for someone to get rid of Becket. At once four knights rode away; Henry sent a man to stop them, but it was too late, and they murdered Becket in his cathedral. Becket was later made a saint.

to Eleanor of Aquitaine. She was famed for her beauty, and her intelligence and spirit matched Henry's.

Henry's aim was to restore England to what it had been under Henry I. He retook lost territories, and destroyed castles, built without permission. He improved the economy and legal system, creating the *Curia Regis*, or King's Court, which travelled around the country so that **freemen** could seek justice there. He also founded a system of six travelling **assizes**. He introduced trial by jury, and began the use of Westminster as a centre of government.

Oxford University. In 1167 Oxford became important as a centre of learning, when the University of Paris banned English students.

Henry was not so good as a father, and his sons became discontented with their lack of power and plotted against him. His marriage to Eleanor had turned sour, and she joined her favourite son, Richard, in plotting against Henry. In 1173, after Eleanor had aided three of their sons in a rebellion, Henry placed her in honourable confinement. There she remained until Henry's death.

In 1183 Henry's heir, 'Young King' Henry, died. Richard, Eleanor's favourite, was now the eldest, and the natural heir. But Henry would not proclaim him heir, nor let him go on Crusade. Richard was angry. He enlisted the help of King Philip II of France, and attacked his father's French territories. When Henry, ill and exhausted from fighting, learnt that his favourite son, John, had joined Richard, he died, broken-hearted.

Henry's queen, Eleanor of Aquitaine. Eleanor was famed for her beauty, brilliant mind, and courage.

RICHARD I
(Coeur-de-lion)
1189-1199 (b. 1157)

RICHARD I

Richard was handsome, brave, tall and strong. Because of his bravery in battle, he became known as 'Coeur-de-lion', meaning 'Lion-heart'.

His first action as king was to free his mother Eleanor, and send her to England to rule until he arrived from France. Richard was crowned in September 1189, and left England that December, as co-leader of the Third Crusade. England was mainly a source of money for Richard's military exploits. He was hero-worshipped for his fighting ability, and because Crusaders were thought of as heroic, noble, and close to God. In fact, Richard behaved with great savagery whilst fighting the Muslims.

Eleanor, Richard's mother, and Richard's ransom. This pile of treasure was the 150,000 marks (35 tons) the English raised to buy Richard out of captivity in Austria.

A fictional picture of Richard fighting Saladin. In reality they never met.

In 1191 Richard and his army besieged the city of Acre, in Palestine. Richard was keen to move on to Jerusalem, and lost patience while waiting for a ransom to be paid. So he chained up all 3,000 citizens of Acre, including women and children, and ordered them to be slaughtered. Saladin, the leader of the Muslims, was a man of honour and had never committed so cruel an act.

After the Third Crusade, Richard hurried to France to defend his territories there. He loved, but did not trust, his brother John. Richard gave John land in Normandy, and **revenues** in England, to satisfy John's thirst for power and wealth. Even so, John tried to overthrow Richard's government, but received no support from the barons, who admired Richard. John then supported Richard against King Philip II of France.

Richard spoke only French, and spent no more than six months of the ten years of his reign in England. He died in France of gangrene from an arrow wound in the shoulder.

These unlucky omens shadowed Richard's reign:
1 His father's corpse bled at the nose when he neared it. It was said that a corpse bled only in the presence of its murderer.
2 A bat flew around him in daylight at his coronation.
3 His sacred Crusader's staff broke when he leaned upon it.

JOHN (Lackland)
1199-1216 (b. 1167)

Part of a painting of King John hunting. John loved hunting. He took away the rights of his subjects to hunt or grow food in the royal forests, so that he could hunt in peace. This increased the barons' anger.

JOHN

John was unpopular because of his history of plotting against family members and betraying allies. He was not glamorous, or religious, or a great warrior. He inherited a kingdom made penniless by Richard I's expensive foreign wars.

John did not do much to improve matters, but he did run the government very efficiently. He cared about just laws, especially for poor people.

In 1208 John rejected the Pope's choice, Stephen Langton, as Archbishop of Canterbury. In anger, the Pope banned all religious rites in England, except for baptism and **last rites**. In response, John seized church property and wealth. In 1209, as punishment for this, the Pope **excommunicated** John, and in 1213 told King Philip II of France to invade England. At this, John gave in and finally swore obedience to the Pope, who lifted his ban. Stephen Langton's first act as Archbishop was to lift John's excommunication.

John was unlucky in war. He lost most of England's land in France, and so he lived up to his nickname, 'Lackland'. The powerful barons had had enough. They hated John's

In 1215 John signed a treaty with the barons. It was later called the 'Magna Carta' (which is Latin for 'Great Charter'). It is famous because it included a promise that all people should have the right to justice. Never before had a king of England signed such a treaty.

heavy taxes, especially **scutage**, and in 1214 they rose against him. In 1215, in a meadow by the River Thames called Runnymede, John signed a treaty with the barons. A few months later, John persuaded the Pope to release him from the promises made in the treaty. The barons were still very angry and fought John. In 1216, exhausted with fighting, John died of a fever.

A jewelled cup, part of John's treasures lost in 1216 when some baggage wagons fell into the Nene estuary. It was recently recovered.

HENRY III
1216-1272 (b. 1207)

William Marshal's tomb in the Temple Church, London. Marshal was famed throughout the Christian world for his courage, physical power and skill in fighting, and also for his honourable nature. He served Henry II, Richard I and John with utter loyalty. Peers and churchmen alike respected his wisdom and asked his advice. Finally, in his 70s, he ruled as Regent for the boy-king, Henry III.

HENRY III

Henry was only nine years old when he became king. So William Marshal, Earl of Pembroke, acted as **Regent** until his death in 1219, when another Regent took over until 1227. They ruled the country for the young Henry. Marshal was a giant in strength, sense, and loyalty. He had been the little hostage whose life King Stephen had spared (see page 21). Strong in battle, and a loving and unselfish servant, he served Henry II, Richard I, and John with great loyalty.

Unfortunately, Henry was a weak king, foolish and dishonourable. Unlucky in war, he failed to regain England's territories in France, lost by King John.

Henry's wife, Eleanor, was French. She brought French nobles to the English court. Henry showed special favour to these Frenchmen, often giving them English land. This made them hated by the English barons. The high taxes Henry demanded, and his wasting money on useless wars, made things even worse.

In 1258 Simon de Montfort, Henry's brother-in-law, led the barons in demanding changes in the government. De Montfort

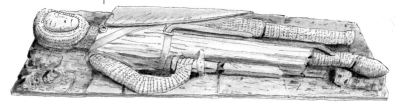

Simon de Montfort's government, the 'Forma Regiminis'. He introduced the 'Council of Nine'. These nine people advised the king. Ordinary citizens took part in government for the first time.

insisted that Henry banish his French favourites. Henry promised to meet these demands, called 'the Provisions of Oxford'.

In 1261 the Pope gave Henry permission to break his promise, and in 1264 civil war broke out. Henry was captured and Simon de Montfort ruled, until he was killed in 1265 in battle with Prince Edward, Henry's son.

Prince Edward was now more powerful in reality than his father, and his promises of fair government, through a parliament, had brought him supporters in the fight against de Montfort. In practice, Edward now became ruler of the country.

Henry spent his last years enjoying his happy and long marriage, and encouraging the arts. He was a lover of architecture and many beautiful cathedrals were built or improved during his reign. Westminster Abbey was rebuilt and Edward the Confessor's remains were reburied there.

Henry overseeing the rebuilding of Westminster Abbey, late in his reign. The Abbey has been central to the history of England. Every English monarch since William I has been crowned there.

EDWARD I
(Longshanks)
1272-1307 (b. 1239)

Edward I was a fine warrior, and won the respect of his subjects. He was very tall and strong, and his nickname, 'Longshanks', referred to his long legs.

He had helped his father, Henry III, to govern since he was twelve, and he had also been a Crusader. He stamped out corruption in government, and in 1295 established a 'Model Parliament' – the first to include clergy, nobles, and commoners. He also changed the legal system.

In 1282 Edward defeated and killed the Welsh prince, Llywelyn, the last of the Welsh royal line. As a recompense, it is said, Edward offered his baby son (also called Edward) to the Welsh people as their prince, at Caernarfon Castle in 1284.

Conwy Castle. The conquest of Wales took five years. Edward made sure of his victory by building fortress castles there, such as this one.

Edward showing his baby son to the Welsh people. This may not really have happened, but it is said that Edward promised the Welsh 'a prince who speaks no English'; the baby Edward could not yet speak at all. In 1301 the young prince was officially created Prince of Wales.

In 13th-century Europe, hatred of Jewish people reached a peak. (The Jews were blamed for Jesus' death, although Jesus was Jewish.) Jews were banned from most jobs and so often became money lenders. English kings relied on them for funds. But Edward I found money elsewhere, and in 1290 he expelled the 3,000 English Jews and took their land.

Edward was determined to conquer Scotland as well as Wales. He gained the title 'Hammer of the Scots', fighting the Scots from 1296 until his death.

Persecution of Jews, from a 13th-century picture. Jews had to wear yellow badges to mark them out.

EDWARD II
1307-1327 (b. 1284)

The unfortunate Edward II was neither wise nor popular. He had no military success, in Scotland or France, and his favouritism towards the handsome Frenchman, Piers Gaveston, infuriated the nobles. Edward even left the rude Gaveston in charge in his place in 1308 while he went to marry Isabella, Princess of France. The barons were so insulted and angry at having Gaveston set above them that they forced Edward to banish him to Ireland. But in 1312 Edward brought him back. There was a revolt in which Gaveston was captured and murdered. In 1321 Edward had new favourites, Hugh Despenser and his power-hungry son, also called Hugh. This caused civil war and

Robert Bruce, the Scottish king at the Battle of Bannockburn, 1314. Bruce's victory there assured Scottish independence. Throughout the rest of Edward's reign, Bruce and his armies attacked northern England.

Edward and Piers Gaveston. Edward was not interested in governing; he preferred sports, or gardening, in the company of his favourite, Gaveston. He even gave Gaveston some of his wedding presents, which hurt his wife's feelings.

Parliament banished the Despensers. Edward won a battle in 1322, and foolishly executed the opposition leader, the Earl of Lancaster (this was the first time a **peer** had been executed).

In 1325 Queen Isabella went to France, and returned with her lover, Roger Mortimer, and an army. They killed the Despensers, imprisoned Edward, and proclaimed the king's young son 'Keeper of the Realm'. Edward II **abdicated** and his son (also called Edward) became king. Mortimer, it is said, saw to it that Edward II was horribly murdered, with a red-hot poker.

*Hungry people were forced to leave their homes, as crop failures in 1314 and 1315 brought **famine**. Food shortages and high prices lasted until 1318.*

EDWARD III

EDWARD III
1327-1377 (b. 1312)

Edward claimed the throne of France and added the French fleur-de-lys symbol on his coat of arms.

The Black Death (bubonic plague) swept England, and the rest of Europe, from 1348 to 1350; one in three people died. The plague was spread by fleas from black rats. This is a 14th-century picture of plague victims being burned.

Edward III took over the government of England from Isabella, his mother, and Roger Mortimer in 1330. His first concern was to avenge his father's shameful death. He executed Mortimer, and compelled Isabella to spend the rest of her days at Castle Rising, in Norfolk.

Edward's reign was a long and great one. He reformed the law, improving justice for ordinary people. He made English, not French, the official language of law and Parliament. He was successful in war, regaining almost a quarter of France, with the help of his warrior son Edward, the Black Prince (so called because he wore black armour). King Edward's determination to claim the French throne (he was nephew of the French king Charles IV, who had no

Edward daydreaming of Arthur's knights. He wanted to create a court like that of the legendary King Arthur, with a Round Table where all were equal and courage, honour, and kindness to the weak were valued above all else.

children) brought about the beginning of the **Hundred Years War** (1337-1453).

One of the main reasons for Edward's military success was the use of the longbow. Only English archers had it. In 1346 the brilliance of the longbowmen brought England victory at the Battle of Crécy, France. Because of this, Calais surrendered to Edward in 1347. The first English gold coin was minted in celebration.

By 1374 only Calais and a tiny strip of southwestern France remained in English hands. Edward did make a few gains in Scotland. He captured the Scots king, David. David was ransomed by his people, and kept the peace with Edward. The Black Prince died in 1376, and his heartbroken father died the following year.

The badge of the knightly 'Order of the Garter'. When a court lady's garter fell off as she danced, Edward stopped people's laughter by picking it up, putting it on his leg, and saying 'Honi soit qui mal y pense' ('Shame on him who thinks badly of it'). He created the Order, with those words as its motto.

RICHARD II
1377-1399 (b. 1367)

Geoffrey Chaucer, author of 'The Canterbury Tales'. He was one of Richard's friends. In his great book, pilgrims travelling to Canterbury each tell a comical tale.

Richard, son of Edward the Black Prince, was another weak king, though he was brave, and showed skill in dealing with other rulers. He brought peace to Ireland, and made a truce with France. He was also a lover of the arts. His big failings were a hasty temper, and the belief that God had made him king and so he could do as he liked.

Richard was only ten when he became king, and his uncle, John of Gaunt, governed as Regent until 1389. In 1397 Richard made himself 'absolute monarch', taking power away from Parliament. In 1399 he went too far when he banished his cousin Henry Bolingbroke, (John of Gaunt's son) and

The pilgrims on their way to Canterbury.

took Henry's inheritance after John of Gaunt's death. Henry returned from France with an army, imprisoned Richard, and forced him to abdicate. Richard was an only child, and had no children. The next in line to the throne, Edmund Mortimer, was only eight. Parliament declared Henry as the next king.

In 1400, a revolt by Richard's supporters was put down.

Following this, Richard was imprisoned in Pontefract Castle and murdered there. He was the last Plantagenet king.

*Richard calms the furious peasants. A high **poll tax**, introduced in 1380, led to the Peasants' Revolt of 1381. The revolt, led by a man named Wat Tyler, ended when Richard spoke to the angry crowd who poured through London, looting and burning.*

*When the Lord Mayor killed Wat Tyler in trying to arrest him, the 14-year-old Richard showed enormous courage. He rode into the angry crowd alone, leading the people away with him, and so prevented a **massacre**.*

**HENRY IV
(Bolingbroke)**
1399-1413 (b. 1367)

HENRY IV

Henry IV was a well-educated, good-mannered man, who loved reading. But his reign was bloody and difficult. It began with the murder of his cousin (Richard II). The first crisis of his reign was a revolt led by the dead Richard's half-brother.

As king, Henry had to deal with rebellions in Wales and Scotland. Owain Glyndwr, the Welsh leader, revolted. So did the Earl of Northumberland, and his son Harry Percy (known as 'Hotspur' because of his temper and love of war). In 1403 Hotspur and his father led an uprising against Henry, who owed them money. Owain Glyndwr and Hotspur were related by marriage, and planned to join forces. Henry was determined to prevent this. Hotspur was killed at the Battle of Shrewsbury.

Henry could hardly afford all this costly fighting. To make it worse, Henry's enemies helped one another, and in 1405 the King of France invaded, along with Glyndwr. Henry resisted them all, but in 1405

Sheep farmers at work shearing. A fall in wool prices created problems for Henry. The tax on these exports had been one of the main sources of royal income.

Owain Glyndwr, the Welsh leader. Glyndwr was a thorn in Henry's side. He was proclaimed Prince of Wales in 1400, and led a revolt that year. He supported the Earl of Northumberland's uprising in 1403, and helped the French to invade in 1405. In 1408 Henry, Prince of Wales, killed Glyndwr's ally, Northumberland. In 1410 Glyndwr abandoned his rebellion.

he became ill. From then on, his son Henry, Prince of Wales, and a fine soldier, took more responsibility, defeating and executing the Earl of Northumberland in 1408, and governing from 1409.

Henry's illness scarred his skin and paralysed him. Many believed it was God's punishment for the murder of Richard II. Henry felt guilty about Richard's death, and spent many hours praying in Westminster Abbey, at the tomb of Edward the Confessor.

HENRY V
1413-1422 (b. 1387)

HENRY V

Henry V was loved and honoured by his people. Like his father (Henry IV), he loved the arts. He showed great self-discipline and was astoundingly successful in war, and very religious. He was generous to his father's opponents, and reburied the murdered Richard II with honour.

Henry's personality changed when he became king; he had led a wild, fun-loving life as Prince of Wales. As king, he behaved in a sensible, thoughtful, dignified, and mature manner. Henry's reign began with plots against him, but the conspirators were caught and executed. He continued the Hundred Years War against France, begun by Edward III. In 1415, Henry and his army sailed to France. They captured the town of Harfleur in September. By October they were exhausted. Many were ill and they

The English longbow. It was much faster than the French crossbow.

Agincourt, 1415. This battle has made Henry immortal. He so inspired his men, an army mostly of archers, that they shattered the resistance of a huge French force.

had very little food left.

Henry was a brilliant leader. He arranged his army so intelligently, and inspired them so powerfully, that at the Battle of Agincourt, near Calais, they defeated a mounted French army three to five times the size of the English force. Only about 500 English soldiers were killed, compared with about 7,000 French soldiers.

More brilliant victories followed, until in 1419 the French king made peace. The two kings signed a treaty, which allowed Henry to keep all the land he had conquered. It also gave him the French king's daughter, Catherine, in marriage, and said Henry should become the next King of France.

= English possessions in France in 1422.

The victorious Henry forces King Charles VI of France to make him heir to the French throne in 1420. Henry died before he could be crowned King of France.

HENRY VI
1422-1461
1470-1471 (b. 1421)

The Wars of the Roses were fought from 1455 to 1485, between the Lancastrians (whose badge was a red rose) and the Yorkists (whose badge was a white rose).

HENRY VI

Henry VI, son of Henry V, was only a baby when he came to the throne. His great-uncle acted as Regent until Henry was crowned king when he was nine years old.

Henry was better fitted to be a monk than a king. His reign was a chapter of disasters. England lost almost all her French territories again. This caused such anger that in 1450 the common people rebelled, led by a man named Jack Cade.

Margaret of Anjou

Most disastrous for Henry, in 1455 the battle for the throne began between the Houses of Lancaster and York. Henry was the great-grandson of Edward III's son, John of Gaunt. John's son had been Duke of Lancaster. But Edmund Mortimer was descended through a female line, from an older son of Edward III and he thought *he* should be king. Many supported him. Mortimer's nephew, Edward, Duke of York, fought against Henry. This struggle, later called the Wars of the Roses, continued, on and off, for the next thirty years.

Henry's queen, Margaret of Anjou, was a good leader. She led Henry's forces against the Yorkists with courage and vigour. But Henry was captured twice, and in 1461 he was deposed, in favour of Edward, Duke of York, who had himself crowned Edward IV.

After being deposed, Henry wandered the country in exile, until in 1470 Margaret returned with an army, and captured King Edward. Henry VI became king for the second time, but the people were against him. In 1471 he was again deposed after a defeat at the Battle of Tewkesbury, where his son was killed. The king was imprisoned in the Tower of London, and murdered there.

Joan of Arc. This peasant girl who had visions of freedom for France led the French armies to victory over Henry's men at Orléans in 1429. In 1431 French churchmen who supported the English burnt her at the stake as a witch.

Henry sings and dances under a tree during a battle. In 1453 Henry had a period of madness. He wore humble clothes, disliking the grandeur of royal show.

Edward IV was another tall, handsome, warrior king. The scheming Earl of Warwick had helped Edward to the throne by deposing Henry VI in 1461. Warwick did not like Edward's wife, Elizabeth Woodville, who was a commoner. Nor did he like the power Edward gave to her family, so he betrayed Edward and helped Queen Margaret to restore her husband, Henry VI, to the throne in 1470. Edward defeated them at the Battle of Barnet. Henry VI was murdered soon afterwards.

Edward IV returned to the throne, and the rest of his reign was peaceful and prosperous, for him and for England.

Edward V had almost no reign. His so-called 'Protector', his uncle Richard of Gloucester, declared Edward's parents' marriage invalid, which made the young king appear to be illegitimate. Richard said the 12-year-old Edward should not be king. Richard was made king instead. Edward and his younger brother were held inside the Tower of London. The two children were seen playing there until July 1483, when they disappeared.

Richard III's reign was short, and shadowed by the terrible suspicion that he had had his little nephews murdered. It seemed only a matter of time

EDWARD IV
1461-1470
1471-1483 (b. 1442)
EDWARD V
Apr-June 1483 (b. 1470)
RICHARD III
1483-1485 (b. 1452)

A printing press. William Caxton set up the first press in 1476. Printing completely changed society.

before Henry Tudor, of the Lancastrian line, would claim the throne. In 1485 Henry Tudor invaded, and met Richard III at the Battle of Bosworth Field. Many of Richard's men deserted, and he was defeated and killed. He had begun his reign betraying his brother and the two nephews entrusted to his care. He ended it fighting bravely, but in shame. His dead body was carted away naked and dirty, slung over a horse's back.

Edward V at confession. His doctor said that Edward confessed and did **penance** *daily, expecting to be killed soon.*

Elizabeth Woodville. She was not of royal blood, but her beauty captured Edward IV's heart. This marriage, of king and commoner, provided the scheming Richard III with an excuse to depose her son, Edward V.

Richard III's body being led away on horseback after the Battle of Bosworth Field, in 1485.

GLOSSARY

abdicate to give up being monarch

Anglo-Saxon a Saxon who inhabited England before the Norman Conquest *or* the language spoken by Anglo-Saxons

assizes courts of law, usually holding regular sessions (or sittings)

counterfeiter a person who forges coins. Severe punishments were handed out to such criminals

Crusades a series of 'Holy Wars' waged by European Christians on Muslims in the 11th-13th centuries, in an attempt to win Jerusalem, the 'holy city' of both religions

Danegeld payments by Saxon rulers to the Vikings to stop them attacking. From 991 rulers raised these payments by taxation. The Norman kings continued to make people pay this tax until 1162

Danelaw the part of England controlled by the Vikings

depose to force a monarch from the throne

devout deeply and faithfully religious

dynasty a ruling family, in which power is passed down by inheritance

earl in Saxon times, a ruler of one of the English 'kingdoms', owing loyalty to the king. As the king's power increased, the power of the earls decreased a little, although they, like other nobles, could and did cause trouble for unpopular kings

excommunicate to expel someone from membership of the Christian Church and ban them from attending services

famine a period of mass starvation, usually resulting from a failure of the usual food supply

feudal society the system introduced by William I, with society divided into classes. Each class worked (or provided soldiers or money) for the one above, in exchange for land and protection

freeman in feudal society, a free man, with legal rights. That is, a member of any class but the lowest

frontier the border of a country or territory

Holy Roman Emperor the ruler of the Holy (that is, Christian) Roman Empire, which covered a large area of Europe

hostage in war, someone given into enemy hands as a guarantee that the hostage-givers will keep an agreement. If they break it, the hostage is killed

Hundred Years War a series of battles between England and France fought during the years from 1337 to 1453, chiefly over parts of France claimed by the English

illegitimate born to parents who were not legally married and, therefore, not entitled to inherit wealth, rank, or property from the father

last rites Christian ritual for a person about to die

massacre killing of a large number of virtually defenceless people at one time

peer (in this book) a nobleman. It can also mean 'an equal'

penance punishment, decreed either by the Church, or by the guilty person, for a sin against religious principles

plunder to rob or steal greedily, especially in war

poll tax a tax payable by every person ('poll' is an old word for 'head', especially used to refer to 'counting heads')

ravage to damage, plunder and terrorise (a country or region)

Regent someone appointed to rule instead of a monarch who is too young, or ill, or out of the country

revenue money coming in regularly; something producing regular money

scutage 'shield tax', a tax that knights and barons had to pay if they did not fight in the king's army

serf (or villein) a member of the lowest class in feudal society. Serfs were not free, were forced to work for their lords, had no legal rights, and could not own land

treaty a written agreement, usually between countries that have been at war

Wessex the ancient West Saxon kingdom, covering most of southwest England. It was the heart of Anglo-Saxon England

INDEX

Kings
of
England

ABOUT FAMILY TREES

This family tree shows the family relationships between English monarchs. You will see that some monarchs were not related by blood to previous monarchs as they took the throne by force.

The dates under each monarch's name indicate when the monarch reigned. By looking at these dates, you can see the order in which the monarchs ruled.

In family trees the eldest child is always shown on the left and the youngest on the right. The eldest child normally rules first. Different coloured lines denote different families or royal houses.

THE SAXON   **KINGS**

Alfred *the Great*
871 – 899

Edward *the Elder*
899 – 924

Athelstan
924 – 939

Edmund *the Magnificent*
939 – 946

Edred
946 – 955